JESUS LOVES YOU

Contact Us:

MyBibleWorkbooks@gmail.com

Projectkingdomcome

Projectkingdomcome

PROJECT KINGDOM COME
ISBN 978-1-961786-11-0

Get The Entire Workbook Series!

SCAN ME

THE BOOK OF
GENESIS
BIBLE-BASED WORKBOOK
Take an adventure into the amazing Book of Genesis and test your knowledge as you go!
PROJECT KINGDOM COME

THE BOOKS OF
EXODUS & JOSHUA
BIBLE-BASED WORKBOOK
Take an adventure into the amazing Books of Exodus and Joshua and test your knowledge as you go!
PROJECT KINGDOM COME

THE BOOKS OF
I & II SAMUEL
BIBLE-BASED WORKBOOK
Take an adventure into the amazing Books of 1st and 2nd Samuel and test your knowledge as you go!
PROJECT KINGDOM COME

THE BOOKS OF
I & II KINGS
BIBLE-BASED WORKBOOK
Take an adventure into the amazing Books of 1st and 2nd Kings and test your knowledge as you go!
PROJECT KINGDOM COME

THE BOOKS OF
ESTHER & RUTH
BIBLE-BASED WORKBOOK
Take an adventure into the amazing Books of Esther and Ruth and test your knowledge as you go!
PROJECT KINGDOM COME

THE BOOKS OF
DANIEL & JOB
BIBLE-BASED WORKBOOK
Take an adventure into the amazing Books of Daniel and Job and test your knowledge as you go!
PROJECT KINGDOM COME

THE BOOK OF
MATTHEW
BIBLE-BASED WORKBOOK
Take an adventure into the amazing Book of Matthew and test your knowledge as you go!
PROJECT KINGDOM COME

THE BOOK OF
MARK
BIBLE-BASED WORKBOOK
Take an adventure into the amazing Book of Mark and test your knowledge as you go!
PROJECT KINGDOM COME

THE BOOK OF
LUKE
BIBLE-BASED WORKBOOK
Take an adventure into the amazing Book of Luke and test your knowledge as you go!
PROJECT KINGDOM COME

THE BOOK OF
JOHN
BIBLE-BASED WORKBOOK
Take an adventure into the amazing Book of John and test your knowledge as you go!
PROJECT KINGDOM COME

THE BOOK OF
ACTS
BIBLE-BASED WORKBOOK
Take an adventure into the amazing Book of Acts and test your knowledge as you go!
PROJECT KINGDOM COME

THE BOOK OF
REVELATION
BIBLE-BASED WORKBOOK
Take an adventure into the amazing Book of Revelation and test your knowledge as you go!
PROJECT KINGDOM COME

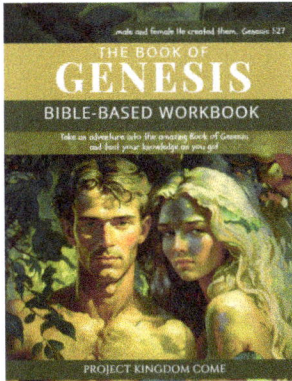

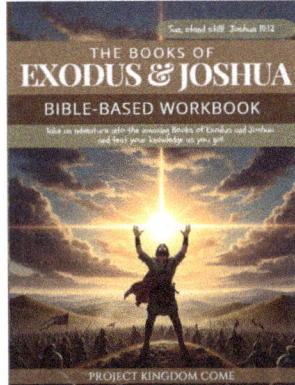

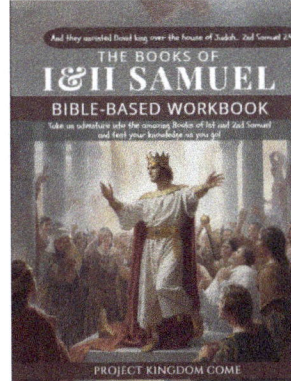

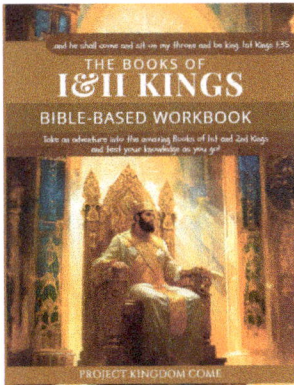

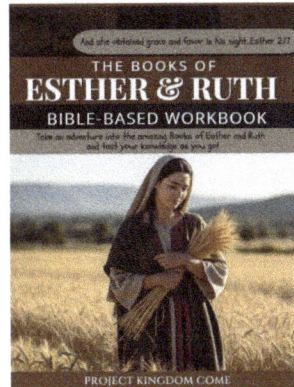

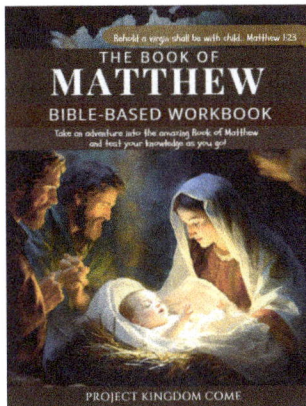

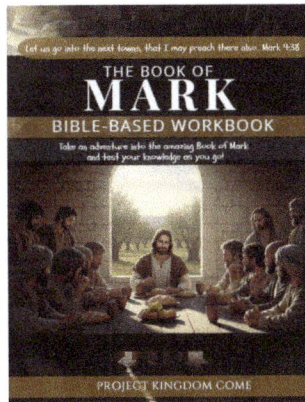

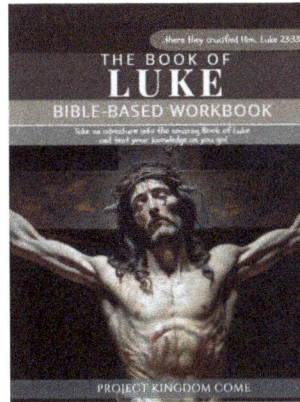

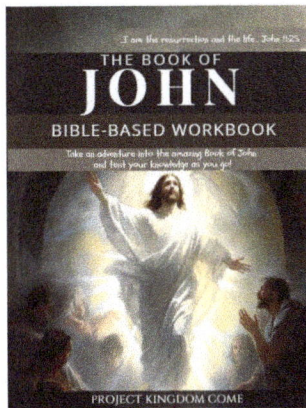

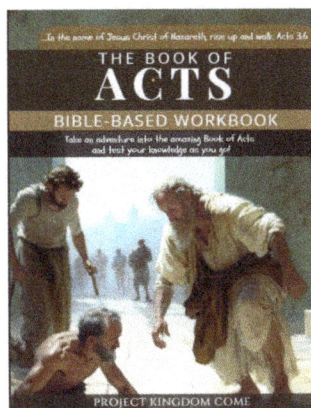

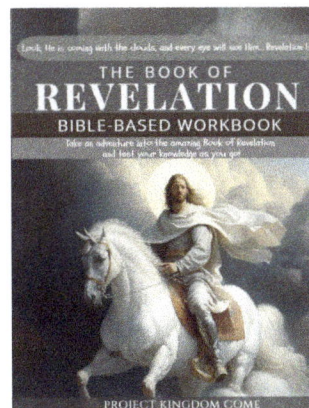

WWW.MYBIBLEWORKBOOKS.COM

PROJECT KINGDOM COME

This workbook belongs to:

_____

_____

_____

Leave your mark!

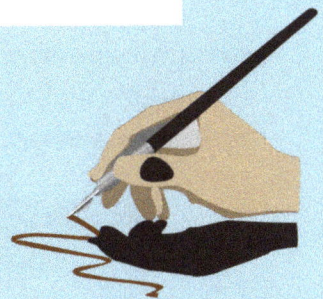

HOW TO USE THIS WORKBOOK

This workbook is designed to help young people explore the treasures in God's Word while having fun, growing in faith, and learning how to search the Scriptures for life's answers.

Here is what you will find inside:

Multiple Choice Questions
Each question comes directly from Scripture and includes a reference verse to help with locating the answer in the Bible. If possible, use a physical Bible to search for the answers.

Weekly Segments
Questions are grouped in weekly categories that could also be completed in a shorter or longer time frame.

Weekly Memory Verses
At the start of every week is a Bible verse to memorize. Each day of that week will repeat that memory verse with a chance to test memorization at the end of the week.

Certificate of Completion
At the end of the workbook, please find a Certificate of Achievement, ready for the child's name and parent or teacher's signature. Celebrate the accomplishment of studying an entire book in the Bible!

Answer Key
The workbook contains an answer key to serve as a support tool for parents or teachers reviewing the responses.

Recommendation for Parents and/or Teachers: Review the responses with your child or student and discuss lessons learned or interesting insights, to improve the child's retention and enrichment in the knowledge of God's word.

> You can do all things through Christ who gives you strength!
> Philippians 4:13

SAMPLE QUESTION...

HOW TO USE THIS WORKBOOK

Reading the reference verse will always lead you to the correct answer!

In the beginning was: (John 1:1)

(A) The Word
B. Heaven and Earth
C. Heaven only
D. Earth only

The number that comes after the book is the 'Chapter'

This is the name of a book in the Bible

John 1:1

The number after the chapter is the 'Verse'

NOW TEST YOURSELF! FIND JOSHUA CHAPTER 1 VERSE 8 IN YOUR BIBLE!

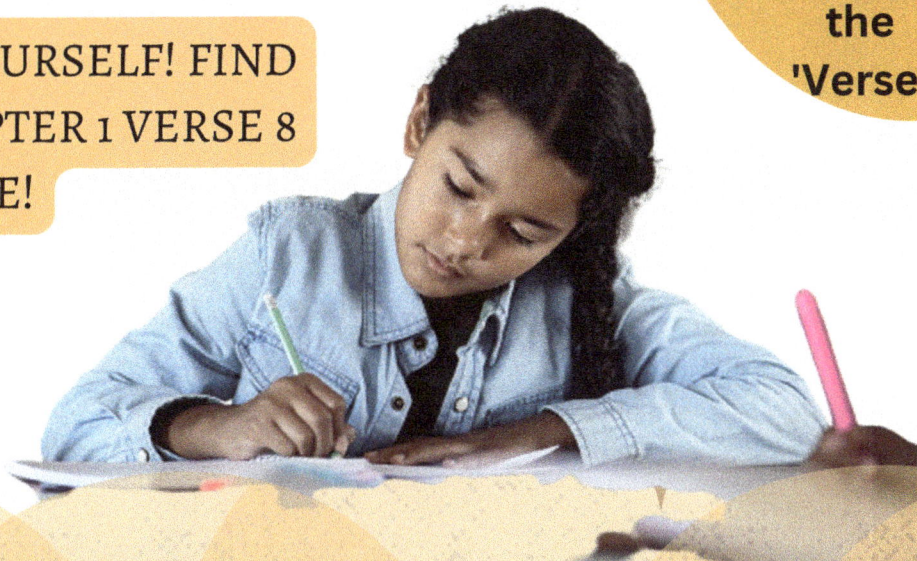

INTRODUCTION: THE BOOK OF REVELATION

The Final Word: Jesus Wins!

The **Book of Revelation** is the final book of the Bible, and it's not just a conclusion; it's a **glorious unveiling of Jesus Christ in all His power, majesty, and victory.**

Written by the **Apostle John** while exiled on the island of Patmos, Revelation is a **prophetic vision of what is, what was, and what is yet to come.**

This book is filled with vivid imagery, symbols, and heavenly scenes that point to one truth: **Jesus is King of kings and Lord of lords, and in the end, He triumphs over all evil.**

Though some parts may seem mysterious, Revelation is not meant to confuse us—it's meant to **strengthen our faith, warn us of spiritual deception, and remind us to stay faithful until the very end.**

As you go through this workbook, you will:
- **Discover what Jesus said to the seven churches**
- **Understand the meaning behind the scroll, the seals, the trumpets, and the bowls**
- **Witness the final defeat of Satan, the beast, and all darkness**
- **Be inspired by the hope of a new heaven, a new earth, and eternal life with God**

Revelation is not just a book about the end; it's a book of new beginnings, of eternal promises, and of the unshakable victory of Jesus Christ.

As you study it, may your heart burn with boldness, reverence, and joyful hope!

"Behold, He is coming with clouds, and every eye will see Him..." - Revelation 1:7

WEEK 1

1. According to Revelation 1:1, what is the purpose of the revelation from Jesus Christ? (Revelation 1:1)

A. To show that God is the creator of all things
B. To explain all the stories and parables in the Gospels
C. To show His servants what must soon take place
D. To show people that Jesus is a revealer of all things

2. How did God make the revelation known? (Revelation 1:1)

A. He sent His angel to His servant John
B. He showed it to Abraham in a dream
C. He wrote it on a tablet and gave it to Moses
D. He made a sign in the clouds for Joshua to see

3. What blessing is promised in Revelation 1:3? (Revelation 1:3)

A. There are blessings for reading the Book of Revelation
B. There are blessings for hearing and keeping what is written in the Book of Revelation
C. Both A and B are correct
D. None of the answers are correct

WEEK 1 MEMORY VERSE: REVELATION 1:8
"I am the Alpha and the Omega, the Beginning and the End," says the Lord, "who is and who was and who is to come, the Almighty."

4. How many churches is the Book of Revelation written to? (Revelation 1:4)

A. 144
B. 12
C. 10
D. 7

5. How many spirits are before God's throne? (Revelation 1:4)

A. 1
B. 7
C. 1000
D. They cannot be counted

6. According to Revelation 1:5, how has Jesus freed us from our sins? (Revelation 1:5)

A. By His blood
B. By His anointing
C. Through our good actions
D. By punishment

WEEK 1 MEMORY VERSE: REVELATION 1:8
"I am the Alpha and the Omega, the Beginning and the End," says the Lord, "who is and who was and who is to come, the Almighty."

7. How many people will see Jesus when He comes back with the clouds? (Revelation 1:7)

A. Only those who believe in Him
B. Only those who don't believe
C. Only people who are awake
D. Everyone - every eye will see Him

8. Which of the following is NOT true about Jesus? (Revelation 1:8)

A. He is the Alpha and the Omega
B. He is the one who was, who is, and who is to come
C. He is the Almighty God
D. He is the son of Saul

9. Where was John when he heard the loud voice like a trumpet? (Revelation 1:9–10)

A. On the edge of the Jordan River
B. On the Island of Patmos
C. In Bethlehem
D. In Jerusalem

WEEK 1 MEMORY VERSE: REVELATION 1:8
"I am the Alpha and the Omega, the Beginning and the End," says the Lord, "who is and who was and who is to come, the Almighty."

WEEK 1

10. Which churches received messages in Revelation? (Revelation 1:11)

A. Matthew, Mark, Luke, John, Andrew, Peter, James
B. Ephesians, Romans, Corinthians, Philippians, Jude, Acts, Hebrews
C. Ephesus, Smyrna, Pergamum, Thyatira, Sardis, Philadelphia, Laodicea
D. All the above

11. What did John see when he turned to hear the voice? (Revelation 1:12–13)

A. 7 golden lampstands and someone like a Son of Man
B. The sun, moon, rainbow, and 15 stars
C. A mighty warrior with wings and golden hair
D. A burning bush speaking

12. Which description is NOT correct about the man speaking to John? (Revelation 1:12–16)

A. He had a golden sash and hair white as snow
B. Eyes like fire, feet like glowing bronze, voice like rushing waters
C. Seven stars in His hand, a sword from His mouth, shining face
D. He had big muscles, was tall, with 7 arrows and a spear

13. What did the man say when John fell at His feet? (Revelation 1:17–18)

A. "Go and tell Pharaoh to let my people go!"

B. "Your wife is going to have a son, and you will name him Isaac."

C. "Silver and gold I do not have, but in the name of Jesus, rise up and walk."

D. "Do not be afraid, I am the First and the Last, I am the Living One. I was dead and now look, I live forever and ever! I hold the keys of death and Hades."

14. When will the things John saw happen? (Revelation 1:19)

A. They happened before Jesus was born

B. They will take place later (in the future)

C. They already happened in the garden of Eden

D. None of those things will ever happen

15. What did Jesus have against the church of Ephesus? (Revelation 2:4)

A. They had forsaken their first love

B. They stopped praise and worship

C. They weren't attending church

D. They brought idols into God's house

WEEK 1 MEMORY VERSE: REVELATION 1:8
"I am the Alpha and the Omega, the Beginning and the End," says the Lord, "who is and who was and who is to come, the Almighty."

16. What reward is promised to the one who overcomes in Ephesus? (Revelation 2:7)

A. They will be made king of a nation
B. They will be made leaders of armies
C. They will have the right to eat from the Tree of Life in God's paradise
D. They will receive great wealth and a long life.

17. What warning was given to the church of Smyrna? (Revelation 2:10)

A. The devil will cause many deaths among them
B. The devil will bring natural disasters to their City
C. The devil will put some of them in prison to test them, and they will suffer for 10 days
D. The devil will inflict them with many sicknesses

18. What is Jesus' promise to the overcomer in Smyrna? (Revelation 2:10)

A. Angels to protect him
B. Blessings each day
C. Joy and happiness
D. The crown of life

WEEK 1 MEMORY VERSE: REVELATION 1:8
"I am the Alpha and the Omega, the Beginning and the End," says the Lord, "who is and who was and who is to come, the Almighty."

19. What is NOT true about the sins of Pergamum? (Revelation 2:14–15)

A. They follow Balaam's teaching
B. Balaam taught sin through idol food and immorality
C. They followed the Nicolaitans
D. They brought idols to church to worship

20. What is Jesus' promise to the overcomer in Pergamum? (Revelation 2:17)

A. Wealth and riches
B. A white stone with a new name, known only to the one who receives it
C. A royal robe and crown
D. A place in Heaven

21. What did Jesus have against the church of Thyatira? (Revelation 2:20)

A. They refused to share their possessions with the poor
B. They tolerated Jezebel, who misled God's servants into sin
C. They celebrated Egyptian and Babylonian festivals
D. They were too proud to seek God

WEEK 1 MEMORY VERSE: REVELATION 1:8
"I am the Alpha and the Omega, the Beginning and the End," says the Lord, "who is and who was and who is to come, the Almighty."

"

The Spirit of God lives within me

(Romans 8:9)

"

Great job completing the week!

Did you memorize the daily verse?
Test yourself by writing it here...

_____

_____

_____

_____

_____

_____

Use this space to draw a scene from the Bible or reflect
on something you learned, felt or experienced...

WEEK 2

22. How will Jesus repay each person? (Revelation 2:23)

A. He will repay them based on their faith alone
B. He will repay them according to their deeds
C. He will reward people based on when they became His disciples
D. He will only reward those who have performed miracles

23. What is NOT a reward Jesus promised to the one who overcomes in Thyatira? (Revelation 2:26–29)

A. Authority over the nations
B. Ruling the nations with an iron scepter
C. Receiving the Morning Star
D. Getting a second chance to live on the earth

24. What did Jesus say about the church in Sardis? (Revelation 3:1–2)

A. "You are known for being alive, but you are dead. Wake up!"
B. "You serve other gods. Repent now."
C. "You ignore the poor, so I will spit you out."
D. "I have called you, but you refuse to return."

WEEK 2 MEMORY VERSE: REVELATION 3:20
Behold, I stand at the door and knock. If anyone hears My voice and opens the door,
I will come in to him and dine with him, and he with Me.

WEEK 2

25. How will Jesus come back, according to Revelation 3:3?

A. In the morning, as the Bright Morning Star
B. Like a thief, when no one expects it
C. After prophets tell the people about His coming
D. With a great army and loud trumpets, giving everyone a clear warning

26. What will Jesus give to those who are victorious and have not soiled their clothes? (Revelation 3:4–5)

A. A purple robe and reunion with family
B. They will become like angels
C. A white robe, and their name will never be removed from the Book of Life
D. Special powers to perform miracles in the new earth

27. What is special about the key of David that Jesus holds? (Revelation 3:7)

A. It opens the gates of Hades to set prisoners free
B. It unlocks ancient mysteries about the end times
C. It represents His authority over earthly kings
D. What the Lord Jesus opens with this key, no one can shut, and what He shuts no one can open

WEEK 2 MEMORY VERSE: REVELATION 3:20
Behold, I stand at the door and knock. If anyone hears My voice and opens the door, I will come in to him and dine with him, and he with Me.

WEEK 2

28. What pleased Jesus about the church in Philadelphia? (Revelation 3:8–9)

A. They were full of brotherly love
B. They had little strength but stayed faithful and did not deny the name of the Lord
C. They worshiped early in the morning
D. They shared light and love with everyone

29. What did Jesus say about those from the synagogue of Satan? (Revelation 3:9)

A. They say they are Jews, but they are not, and He will make them fall at the feet of His people and acknowledge that they are the ones He loves
B. They say they follow God, but their hearts are far from Him
C. They claim to be chosen, but do not live by the truth
D. They pretend to worship, but do not honor God's name

30. What will the Lord Jesus do for those who keep His command to persevere? (Revelation 3:10)

A. He will give them strength to stand in the day of trouble
B. He will bless them with wisdom and peace
C. He will keep them from the hour of testing coming on the whole world
D. He will send angels to guide them through difficult times

WEEK 2 MEMORY VERSE: REVELATION 3:20
Behold, I stand at the door and knock. If anyone hears My voice and opens the door, I will come in to him and dine with him, and he with Me.

WEEK 2

31. What did Jesus say about His return? (Revelation 3:11)

A. He will return in the perfect time, according to God's will
B. He has already come once and completed His mission
C. We don't have to worry about His return
D. He is coming soon! We all must hold on to what we have, so no one takes our crown

32. What is Jesus' promise to the one who overcomes in Philadelphia? (Revelation 3:12)

A. He will make them a pillar in the temple of His God, and they will never again leave it
B. He will write on them the name of His God and the name of the city of His God, the New Jerusalem
C. He will write on them His new name
D. All of the above

33. What does Jesus say to the people who are neither hot nor cold, and who think they don't need anything from Him?

A. The Lord is about to spit them out of His mouth
B. He says they think they are rich, but they are actually poor, blind, and naked
C. He tells them to buy gold, white clothes, and ointment so they can truly see and be clean
D. All of the above

WEEK 2 MEMORY VERSE: REVELATION 3:20
Behold, I stand at the door and knock. If anyone hears My voice and opens the door, I will come in to him and dine with him, and he with Me.

WEEK 2

34. What does Jesus do for those He loves? (Revelation 3:19)

A. He rebukes and disciplines them so that they can repent
B. He stores all their earthly blessings in Heaven
C. He gives them a loving family and surrounds them with friends
D. He denies them good things on earth but will reward them in Heaven

35. What is the reward for those who overcome in Laodicea? (Revelation 3:21)

A. They will hear the sound of trumpets & defeat all their enemies
B. They will be given the right to sit with Jesus on His throne
C. They will not suffer shame and reproach
D. They will not suffer from diseases of any kind

36. What is the appearance of the person John saw sitting on heaven's throne? (Revelation 4:3)

A. He looked like Jasper and Ruby with a rainbow surrounding the throne
B. He looked like white clouds gathered tightly with a silver line around them
C. He looked like a tall and mighty warrior with a gold crown on His head
D. He looked like sapphire and emerald, surrounded by a glorious light

WEEK 2 MEMORY VERSE: REVELATION 3:20
Behold, I stand at the door and knock. If anyone hears My voice and opens the door, I will come in to him and dine with him, and he with Me.

WEEK 2

37. How many elders sit around the throne of God? (Revelation 4:4)

A. 7
B. 12
C. 24
D. 72

38. Which of the following did John see when he looked at Heaven's throne? (Revelation 4:4-6)

A. Flashes of lightning and peals of thunder
B. Seven burning lamps, which are the seven Spirits of God
C. A sea of glass, clear like crystal
D. All of the above

39. What do the four living creatures in the center and around the throne look like? (Revelation 4: 6-8)

A. One looked like a lion, another like an ox, another like a man, and another like an eagle
B. Each of the four living creatures had six wings and were covered with eyes
C. Both A and B
D. They were bright and shining, like stars in the sky

WEEK 2 MEMORY VERSE: REVELATION 3:20
Behold, I stand at the door and knock. If anyone hears My voice and opens the door, I will come in to him and dine with him, and he with Me.

WEEK 2

40. What do the four living creatures say continually without stopping? (Revelation 4:8)

A. "You are holy and mighty, O Lord of all!"
B. "Holy, holy, holy is the Lord God Almighty, who was, and is, and is to come"
C. "Worthy is the Lord, the God of Heaven and earth"
D. "Glory to God in the highest, and peace to His people on earth"

41. What do the 24 elders say when they fall down and lay their crowns to worship God? (Revelation 4: 11)

A. "You are worthy, our Lord and God, to receive glory and honor and power, for You created all things and by Your will they were created and have their being"
B. "Amazing grace, how sweet the sound that saved a wretch like me"
C. "Praise the Lord! Praise the Lord! Let the earth hear His voice!"
D. "You are Jehovah Jireh, more than enough in every circumstance"

42. Who is the only One found worthy to open the scroll and break its seals? (Revelation 5:5)

A. Moses
B. John the Baptist
C. David, the man after God's own heart
D. The Lion of the tribe of Judah, the Root of David (Jesus)

WEEK 2 MEMORY VERSE: REVELATION 3:20
Behold, I stand at the door and knock. If anyone hears My voice and opens the door, I will come in to him and dine with him, and he with Me.

"
I am clothed with
strength and dignity
and can laugh at days
to come
(Proverbs 31:25)
"

Great job completing the week!

Did you memorize the daily verse?
Test yourself by writing it here...

_____

_____

_____

_____

_____

Use this space to draw a scene from the Bible or reflect
on something you learned, felt or experienced...

WEEK 3

43. What is the incense in the golden bowls held by the four living creatures and the 24 elders? (Revelation 5:8)

A. Sweet-smelling essential oils
B. Frankincense and Myrrh
C. The prayers of God's people
D. The songs of God's angels

44. How did Jesus, the Lamb of God, purchase people for God? (Revelation 5:9–10)

A. Jesus was slain, and with His blood He paid for people from every tribe, language, and nation
B. Jesus owns everything and was able to pay for people to serve God
C. Jesus used His power to convince people to follow God
D. Jesus is not a lamb

45. How many angels were around the throne of God? (Revelation 5:11)

A. 100
B. 11,000
C. A thousand on the left side and ten thousand on the right
D. Thousands upon thousands and ten thousand times ten thousand

WEEK 3 MEMORY VERSE: REVELATION 4:8
The four living creatures, each having six wings, were full of eyes around and within. And they do not rest day or night, saying: "Holy, holy, holy, Lord God Almighty, Who was and is and is to come!"

WEEK 3

46. Who did John hear saying, "To Him who sits on the throne and to the Lamb be praise and honor and glory and power, forever and ever"? (Revelation 5:13)

A. All the angels that surround the throne of God
B. All the creatures in heaven and on earth and under the earth and in the sea
C. All the people who live on earth
D. The 24 elders

47. What happened when the Lamb opened the first seal? (Revelation 6:1-2)

A. One of the four living creatures spoke with a voice like thunder and said 'Come!'
B. A white horse appeared. Its rider had a bow and was given a crown, then went out to win many battles
C. Both A and B are correct
D. A mighty angel appeared and announced the rider's name

48. What happened when the Lamb opened the second seal? (Revelation 6:3-4)

A. The second living creature said 'Come!'
B. A fiery red horse came out and its rider was given power to take peace from the earth
C. The rider of the red horse was given a large sword
D. All the above are correct

WEEK 3 MEMORY VERSE: REVELATION 4:8
The four living creatures, each having six wings, were full of eyes around and within. And they do not rest day or night, saying: "Holy, holy, holy, Lord God Almighty, Who was and is and is to come!"

WEEK 3

49. What happened when the Lamb opened the third seal? (Revelation 6:5-6)

A. The third living creature said 'Come!'
B. A black horse appeared. Its rider was carrying a pair of scales
C. A voice said, "Two pounds of wheat for a day's wages, and six pounds of barley for a day's wage, and do not damage the oil and the wine!"
D. All the above happened

50. Who was the rider on the pale horse? (Revelation 6:8)

A. Death
B. Famine
C. Suffering
D. Pestilence

51. What did John see when the fifth seal was opened? (Revelation 6:9–10)

A. The seven lamps of God standing before His throne
B. The souls of those who had been killed because of the word of God
C. A woman running from a dragon
D. The sun, moon, and 12 stars shining before God

WEEK 3 MEMORY VERSE: REVELATION 4:8
The four living creatures, each having six wings, were full of eyes around and within. And they do not rest day or night, saying: "Holy, holy, holy, Lord God Almighty, Who was and is and is to come!"

WEEK 3

52. Which of the following did NOT happen when the sixth seal was broken? (Revelation 6:12-15)

A. An earthquake, the sun turned black, and the moon turned red like blood
B. Stars fell to the earth, the heavens rolled away, and mountains were removed
C. The oceans dried up and all creatures died from starvation
D. Everyone, including kings, princes and the mighty hid in caves & mountains

53. Which tribe is NOT listed among the 12 tribes whose foreheads were sealed? (Revelation 7:4-8)

A. The tribe of Rueben
B. The tribe of Manasseh
C. The tribe of Benjamin
D. The tribe of Dan

54. Who are the people with white robes and palm branches standing before the throne and the Lamb and where did they come from? (Revelation 7:9-14)

A. They are all the people who died before Jesus came to earth
B. They came out of the great tribulation and washed their robes in the blood of the Lamb
C. They are the mighty armies of Heaven
D. They are the 144,000 sons of Israel

WEEK 3 MEMORY VERSE: REVELATION 4:8
The four living creatures, each having six wings, were full of eyes around and within. And they do not rest day or night, saying: "Holy, holy, holy, Lord God Almighty, Who was and is and is to come!"

WEEK 3

55. What happened when the seventh seal was opened? (Revelation 8:1)

A. There was a loud sound of thunder across the whole earth
B. There was silence in heaven for about half an hour
C. Everyone in heaven bowed and worshipped God
D. The heavens opened and the angels were ascending and descending

56. What was the name of the star that fell from the sky when the third angel sounded his trumpet? (Revelation 8:10–11)

A. Apollyon
B. Abyss
C. Armageddon
D. Wormwood

57. What happened when the fourth angel sounded his trumpet? (Revelation 8:12)

A. A third of the sun, moon, and stars were struck and turned dark
B. Only a few stars fell from the sky
C. The moon disappeared and the stars became red
D. A third of the sky was filled with smoke

WEEK 3 MEMORY VERSE: REVELATION 4:8
The four living creatures, each having six wings, were full of eyes around and within. And they do not rest day or night, saying: "Holy, holy, holy, Lord God Almighty, Who was and is and is to come!"

WEEK 3

58. Why did the eagle flying through the sky cry out with a loud voice? (Revelation 8:13)

A. To warn the people about falling stars

B. Because the sun had been struck, and darkness covered the earth

C. Because of the three trumpet blasts that were still to come

D. To announce the coming of God's kingdom on earth

59. What came out of the smoke when the Abyss was opened? (Revelation 9:1–4)

A. Fire and smoke covered the land

B. Locusts came out and were allowed to harm those without God's seal

C. Locusts and scorpions attacked the earth

D. Bright clouds rose and covered the skies

60. What will happen in the days after the Abyss is opened? (Revelation 9:6)

A. The sun and moon will stop shining

B. People will run out of food and water

C. People will seek death but will not find it. They will long to die, but death will escape them

D. Angels will walk the earth to help people

WEEK 3 MEMORY VERSE: REVELATION 4:8
The four living creatures, each having six wings, were full of eyes around and within. And they do not rest day or night, saying: "Holy, holy, holy, Lord God Almighty, Who was and is and is to come!"

WEEK 3

61. What is the name of the angel of the Abyss that is king over the locusts? (Revelation 9:11)

A. Leviathan the dragon
B. The Absinth
C. Abaddon or Apollyon (The destroyer)
D. Lucifer or Satan

62. Where are the four angels bound that will be released to kill a third of mankind? (Revelation 9:13-15)

A. The great river Nile
B. The depths of the Red Sea
C. The City of Babylon
D. The great river Euphrates

63. How will one third of mankind die after the four angels are released? (Revelation 9:18–19)

A. Four double-edged swords from the mouths of the angels
B. By three plagues - fire, smoke, and sulfur that will come out of the horses' mouths
C. The stars will fall and destroy one-third of mankind
D. The four angels will cause a great famine, and people will die from hunger

WEEK 3 MEMORY VERSE: REVELATION 4:8
The four living creatures, each having six wings, were full of eyes around and within. And they do not rest day or night, saying: "Holy, holy, holy, Lord God Almighty, Who was and is and is to come!"

"From now on let no one trouble me, for I bear in my body the marks of the Lord Jesus (Galatians 6:17)"

Great job completing the week!

Did you memorize the daily verse?
Test yourself by writing it here...

_____

_____

_____

_____

_____

_____

Use this space to draw a scene from the Bible or reflect on something you learned, felt or experienced...

WEEK 4

64. What happened to the rest of mankind that did not die from the three plagues? (Revelation 9: 20-21)

A. They turned away from sin and refused the mark of the beast
B. They experienced persecution and were rewarded with crowns
C. They still did not repent or stop worshiping demons and idols of gold, silver, bronze, stone, and wood—idols that cannot see or hear or walk
D. They repented but continued to worship their idols

65. Which of the following was John NOT allowed to write about? (Revelation 10: 4-5)

A. The appearance of God in Heaven
B. The meaning of the mark of the beast
C. The things that happened after the seventh trumpet
D. The things spoken by the seven thunders said

66. What did the mighty angel standing on the sea and on the land say? (Revelation 10:5-7)

A. "Run to the mountains and hide from the wrath of the seventh angel!"
B. "There will be no more delay! When the seventh angel sounds his trumpet, the mystery of God will be accomplished."
C. "Woe to the earth, for the trumpet has sounded and the king of darkness is coming!"
D. "Release the horses with red, dark blue, and yellow armor and the lion-headed riders!"

WEEK 4 MEMORY VERSE: REVELATION 12:11
And they overcame him by the blood of the Lamb and by the word of their testimony, and they did not love their lives to the death.

WEEK 4

67. What happened when John ate the little scroll from the angel? (Revelation 10:9–10)

A. It instantly gave him the ability to speak many languages
B. It tasted as sweet as honey in his mouth, but his stomach turned sour
C. His eyes were opened to see greater things in Heaven
D. It caused him to prophesy immediately about the future

68. Which part of the temple was John told NOT to measure? (Revelation 11:1–2)

A. The outer court, because it was given to the Gentiles
B. The temple itself, because it is unholy to measure it
C. The altar of God, reserved for the priests
D. The Holy of Holies, because it is sacred ground

69. For how long will the two witnesses prophesy? (Revelation 11: 3)

A. 1,260 days (3 and ½ years)
B. 7 years before the great tribulation
C. 3 and a half days
D. 24 months

WEEK 4 MEMORY VERSE: REVELATION 12:11
And they overcame him by the blood of the Lamb and by the word of their testimony, and they did not love their lives to the death.

WEEK 4

70. What will the two witnesses have power to do? (Revelation 11:6)

A. To shut the heavens so it will not rain
B. To turn water into blood and strike the earth with plagues
C. All of the above
D. None of the above

71. Which of the following is NOT true about what will happen to the two witnesses? (Revelation 11: 7-12)

A. The beast from the Abyss will attack and kill them
B. Their bodies will lie in the street for 3½ days
C. After 3½ days, they will rise and stand on their feet
D. One will go up to Heaven, and the other will stay to fight Satan

72. What was the appearance of the pregnant woman in John's vision? (Revelation 12:1-2)

A. She was wearing a royal robe and riding a white horse
B. She was shining brightly and holding seven stars with a rainbow overhead
C. She was clothed with the sun, the moon under her feet, and a crown of twelve stars on her head
D. She was wearing sackcloth and riding on a winged horse

WEEK 4 MEMORY VERSE: REVELATION 12:11

And they overcame him by the blood of the Lamb and by the word of their testimony, and they did not love their lives to the death.

73. What did the red dragon do to the stars and the pregnant woman?
(Revelation 12: 3-5)

A. Blew fire at the stars and tried to destroy the child
B. Swept a third of the stars out of the sky and tried to kill the woman's child
C. Crushed the stars and pushed the woman off her horse
D. Blew a trumpet and called the stars to guard the woman

74. Complete this verse: Then war broke out in _____.
(Revelation 12:7)

A. Egypt
B. Sodom and Gomorrah
C. Heaven
D. Hell

75. Who fought and won against the dragon and his angels?
(Revelation 12: 7-9)

A. Gabriel and his angels
B. Jesus and his angels
C. Michael and his angels
D. Adam and his angels

WEEK 4 MEMORY VERSE: REVELATION 12:11
And they overcame him by the blood of the Lamb and by the word of their testimony, and they did not love their lives to the death.

WEEK 4

76. What happened to the great dragon (Satan) and his angels when they tried to fight back? (Revelation 12: 7-9)

A. They lost the battle and also lost their place in heaven
B. They were hurled down to the earth and now lead the whole world astray
C. Both A and B are correct
D. None of the above

77. According to Revelation 12:11, how do the people of God triumph and overcome the devil? (Revelation 12:11)

A. By praying without ceasing and trusting in God's promises
B. By staying in fellowship with other believers and obeying God's Word
C. By the blood of the Lamb and the word of their testimony
D. By singing worship songs and reading the Bible every morning

78. Why is the devil filled with fury? (Revelation 12:12)

A. Because his rebellion caused him to fall from Heaven
B. Because he cannot stop the plans of God
C. Because God's people continue to worship and trust in the Lord
D. Because he knows that his time is short

WEEK 4 MEMORY VERSE: REVELATION 12:11
And they overcame him by the blood of the Lamb and by the word of their testimony, and they did not love their lives to the death.

WEEK 4

79. When the serpent tried to destroy the woman with a river, how did the earth help her? (Revelation 12:15–16)

A. The earth turned to the side and let the water fall away
B. The earth surrounded the woman with mountains for protection
C. The earth soaked up the water until it was gone
D. The earth opened its mouth and swallowed the river

80. Who does the dragon (Satan) war against? (Revelation 12: 17)

A. Only the people who know about him
B. Only the people who do not know about him
C. Only the people who are very spiritual
D. All those who keep God's commands and hold firm to their testimony about Jesus

81. Which of the following describes the Beast that came out of the sea? (Revelation 13:1-3)

A. It had 10 horns, 7 heads, and blasphemous names on its heads
B. It looked like a leopard, had feet like a bear, and a mouth like a lion
C. One of its heads seemed to have a fatal wound that had been healed
D. All of the above

WEEK 4 MEMORY VERSE: REVELATION 12:11
And they overcame him by the blood of the Lamb and by the word of their testimony, and they did not love their lives to the death.

WEEK 4

82. Why did people worship the dragon and the beast? (Revelation 13:4-5)

A. Because the dragon had given the beast authority for 42 months
B. Because the dragon looked powerful and mighty
C. Because the beast gave gifts to its worshipers
D. Because the people were afraid of the dragon

83. Which people will worship the beast? (Revelation 13: 8)

A. All those whose names are not written in the Lamb's Book of Life
B. All the people who already worship Satan as their god
C. Only the people who do not believe that a "Book of Life" exists in heaven
D. Only the people who don't understand that the Beast is not a true god

84. Which of the following is true about the second beast that came out of the earth? (Revelation 13: 11-14)

A. It had two horns like a lamb but spoke like a dragon and made people worship the first beast
B. It performed signs, like calling fire down from heaven
C. It told people to make an image of the first beast
D. All of the above

WEEK 4 MEMORY VERSE: REVELATION 12:11
And they overcame him by the blood of the Lamb and by the word of their testimony, and they did not love their lives to the death.

> I am crowned with glory and honor (Psalm 8:5)

Great job completing the week!

Did you memorize the daily verse?
Test yourself by writing it here...

_____

_____

_____

_____

_____

_____

Use this space to draw a scene from the Bible or reflect
on something you learned, felt or experienced...

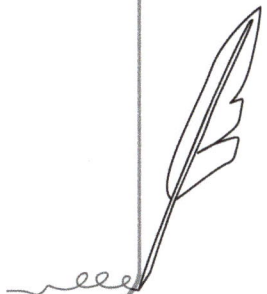

WEEK 5

85. What does the second beast cause to happen?
(Revelation 13:15–17)

A. It gave breath to the image of the first beast so it could speak and order people to be killed
B. It made everyone receive a mark on their right hand or forehead
C. No one could buy or sell unless they had the mark—the name or number of the beast
D. All of the above

86. What is that number of the beast? (Revelation 13:18)

A. 144,000
B. 42
C. 666
D. 7

87. How many stood with the Lamb on Mount Zion, with His name and His Father's name on their foreheads? (Revelation 14:1)

A. 12
B. 144,000
C. 12,000
D. 7

WEEK 5 MEMORY VERSE: REVELATION 19:16
And He has on His robe and on His thigh a name written:
KING OF KINGS AND LORD OF LORDS.

WEEK 5

88. What message did the angel with the eternal gospel give to all people on the earth? (Revelation 14:7)

A. Fear God and give Him glory, for the hour of judgment has come
B. Worship the One who made heaven, earth, sea, and springs of water
C. Both A and B
D. Only A is correct

89. What did the third angel say after the fall of Babylon? (Revelation 14:8–10)

A. Anyone who worships the beast and receives the mark will face God's full wrath
B. They will be tormented with burning sulfur in the presence of the Lamb
C. Their torment will rise forever, and they will have no rest
D. All of the above

90. What tool did the angel sitting on a white cloud use to harvest the earth? (Revelations 14:15-16)

A. Combined harvester
B. Net
C. Sickle
D. A blazing sword

WEEK 5 MEMORY VERSE: REVELATION 19:16
And He has on His robe and on His thigh a name written:
KING OF KINGS AND LORD OF LORDS.

WEEK 5

91. When will God's wrath be complete? (Revelation 15:1)

A. After the last seven plagues
B. After Satan is thrown into the lake of fire
C. When sin and death are defeated
D. When the earth rolls away

92. What instrument did those who were victorious over the beast, its image, and the number of its name use to sing the song of Moses and of the Lamb? (Revelation 15: 2-3)

A. Lyre
B. Harp
C. Trumpet
D. Drum

93. Which of the following correctly describes the seven angels with the seven plagues? (Revelation 15:6)

A. They are dressed in clean, shining linen with golden sashes
B. They have a bright light with stars around their heads
C. They are like glowing sapphire and crystal robes
D. They are dressed in long white robes with purple sashes

WEEK 5 MEMORY VERSE: REVELATION 19:16
And He has on His robe and on His thigh a name written:
KING OF KINGS AND LORD OF LORDS.

WEEK 5

94. Why couldn't anyone enter the temple until the seven plagues were completed? (Revelation 15:8)

A. Because the temple was filled with smoke from the glory of God and from His power.
B. Because they would have been destroyed by the plagues
C. Because God's judgment was not yet completed
D. Because the seventh angel was blocking the entrance

95. What happened when the first bowl of God's wrath was poured out? (Revelation 16:2)

A. Every living thing died, and the moon turned red
B. Painful sores broke out on people who had the mark of the beast
C. The springs of water turned to blood
D. All the earth's water dried up

96. How did people respond to the fourth and fifth bowls of God's wrath? (Revelation 16:8–11)

A. They saw their suffering and turned to God
B. They begged for mercy and removed the mark
C. They cursed God and refused to repent
D. They hid and asked the mountains to fall on them

WEEK 5 MEMORY VERSE: REVELATION 19:16
And He has on His robe and on His thigh a name written:
KING OF KINGS AND LORD OF LORDS.

WEEK 5

97. What happened to the Euphrates River when the sixth bowl was poured out? (Revelation 16:12)

A. Half its water dried up and released angels
B. Its water dried up to prepare the way for kings from the East
C. It turned to blood and killed all fish
D. It overflowed and caused flooding

98. What were the three impure spirits that came from the dragon, beast, and false prophet? (Revelation 16:13–14)

A. Spirits of sin, death, and the grave
B. Principalities, powers, and rulers of darkness
C. Spirits of the antichrist
D. Demonic spirits that performed signs and gathered kings for battle

99. What warning did Jesus give about His return? (Revelation 16:15)

A. He will come like a thief—when no one expects Him
B. Blessed is the one who stays awake and keeps their clothes on, so they won't be ashamed
C. Both A and B
D. None of these, because Jesus won't come unexpectedly

WEEK 5 MEMORY VERSE: REVELATION 19:16
And He has on His robe and on His thigh a name written:
KING OF KINGS AND LORD OF LORDS.

WEEK 5

100. Where will the kings of the earth gather for the great battle? (Revelation 16:16)

A. Jerusalem
B. Gog and Magog
C. Canaan
D. Armageddon

101. What happened when the seventh bowl of God's fierce anger was poured into the air? (Revelation 16: 18-21)

A. A mighty earthquake splits the great city into three parts, and the cities of the nations collapse. Babylon receives the full cup of God's wrath
B. Every island disappears, and the mountains can no longer be found
C. Huge hailstones, each weighing about a hundred pounds, fall on people, and they curse God
D. All the above

102. Why will people whose names are not in the Book of Life be astonished when they see the beast? (Revelation 17:8)

A. Because the beast never existed before, but now will appear
B. Because the beast once was, now is not, and yet will come
C. Because the beast pretended to be strong but will turn out weak
D. Because the beast will reveal its ugly form to all

WEEK 5 MEMORY VERSE: REVELATION 19:16
And He has on His robe and on His thigh a name written:
KING OF KINGS AND LORD OF LORDS.

WEEK 5

103. The woman, Babylon the Great, sits on a scarlet beast with seven heads. What do the seven heads represent? (Revelation 17:9–10)

A. They are seven hills the woman sits on, and also represent seven kings—five have fallen, one is, and one is yet to come
B. They are seven evil spirits that rule the earth
C. They are seven ruling powers that have existed throughout history
D. They represent seven nations that oppose God

104. What does the beast that "once was and now is not" represent? (Revelation 17:10–11)

A. It is Abaddon, the king of the Abyss
B. It is an eighth king who belongs to the seven and will go to his destruction
C. It is the beast that brings the seven plagues
D. It is the enemy who will rise again to deceive the nations.

105. What do the ten horns on the beast represent? (Revelation 17:12)

A. Ten powerful armies that will rise at the end of time
B. Ten regions of the world that will ally with the beast
C. Kings who join the Lord's army at the end
D. Ten kings who have not yet received a kingdom but will share authority with the beast for one hour

WEEK 5 MEMORY VERSE: REVELATION 19:16
And He has on His robe and on His thigh a name written:
KING OF KINGS AND LORD OF LORDS.

> "I have authority to trample on serpents and scorpions, and over all the power of the enemy. And nothing shall by any means hurt me (Luke 10:19)"

Great job completing the week!

Did you memorize the daily verse?
Test yourself by writing it here...

_____

_____

_____

_____

_____

Use this space to draw a scene from the Bible or reflect on something you learned, felt or experienced...

WEEK 6

106. What is the purpose of the ten Kings? (Revelation 17:12-14)

A. To give their power and authority to the beast and make war against the Lamb
B. To help the Lamb win the battle
C. To support the beast in global rebellion against God
D. To spread plagues through the world

107. What will be the outcome of the war between the kings and the Lamb of God? Revelation 17: 14)

A. The war will end the world and cause heaven and earth to vanish
B. The Lamb will conquer because He is Lord of Lords and King of Kings
C. The Lamb will triumph with His chosen, faithful followers
D. Both B and C

108. The prostitute known as Babylon the Great is seen sitting on the waters. What do these waters represent? (Revelation 17:15)

A. The great oceans and seas of the world
B. Peoples, multitudes, nations, and languages
C. The second heaven
D. Religions of the world

WEEK 6 MEMORY VERSE: REVELATION 22:12
And behold, I am coming quickly, and My reward is with Me, to give to everyone according to his work.

WEEK 6

109. Who will God use to bring Babylon the Great to her end? (Revelation 17:16-18)

A. The beast will shoot arrows from its mouth
B. The Lamb and His army
C. The beast and the ten kings will turn against her, eat her flesh, and burn her with fire
D. The seventh angel will pour wrath on her

110. What will Babylon become after her fall? (Revelation 18:2)

A. Babylon will become a dwelling for demons and every evil spirit
B. Babylon will be thrown into the lake of fire
C. Babylon will be renamed the City of Sin
D. Babylon will become a desert that burns for a thousand years

111. How will Babylon be repaid for her evil deeds? (Revelation 18:6)

A. She will be exposed as a liar to all the people and kings who dwell on the earth
B. She will be shown mercy
C. She will be given a chance to repent and then be punished for a thousand years
D. She will be repaid double according to her evil deeds

WEEK 6 MEMORY VERSE: REVELATION 22:12
And behold, I am coming quickly, and My reward is with Me, to give to everyone according to his work.

WEEK 6

112. How long will it take for Babylon the Great to fall? (Revelation 18:10)

A. One hour
B. One Minute
C. One Second
D. One Day

113. What type of things did people buy from Babylon before her fall? (Revelation 18:11–13)

A. Gold, silver, fine linen, silk, pearls
B. Wood, ivory, iron, marble
C. Spices, wine, animals, wheat, oil
D. All the above

114. What else was being sold in Babylon that shows its wickedness? (Revelation 18:13)

A. The pleasures of life
B. Nations and kings
C. Land and inheritances
D. Slaves and the souls of men

WEEK 6 MEMORY VERSE: REVELATION 22:12
And behold, I am coming quickly, and My reward is with Me, to give to everyone according to his work.

WEEK 6

115. Who were the traders in Babylon that were deceived by her sorcery and magic? (Revelation 18:23)

A. The world's important people (great and powerful men)
B. Purple linen and silk traders
C. The ten kings
D. Those who took the mark of the beast

116. What does the fine linen worn by the Bride of the Lamb represent? (Revelation 19: 7-8)

A. Fabric worn in heaven
B. The righteous acts of God's people
C. The glory of God
D. The outfit for those who show mercy

117. Complete this verse: Blessed are those who are invited to the wedding supper of the lamb _____ (Revelation 19: 9)

A. "For they shall see God"
B. "For they shall never hunger or thirst again"
C. "These are the true words of God"
D. "For they will receive eternal life"

WEEK 6 MEMORY VERSE: REVELATION 22:12
And behold, I am coming quickly, and My reward is with Me, to give to everyone according to his work.

WEEK 6

118. What was the angel's response when John fell down to worship him? (Revelation 19: 10)

A. "Don't do that! I am a fellow servant with you…"
B. "Worship God. For the testimony of Jesus is the Spirit of prophecy"
C. "Worship the cross"
D. Both A and B

119. What is the name of the Rider on the white horse? (Revelation 19:11)

A. The King of Kings
B. Faithful and True
C. Emmanuel
D. The Commander of Heaven's Army

120. Which of the following describes the appearance of the rider on the white horse? (Revelation 19: 11-12)

A. His hair falls back in curls that shine like the sun
B. His eyes are like blazing fire and on his head are many crowns
C. He has six wings, and each wing has eyes all over them
D. His arms are like polished gold and his face is radiant

WEEK 6 MEMORY VERSE: REVELATION 22:12
And behold, I am coming quickly, and My reward is with Me, to give to everyone according to his work.

WEEK 6

121. What is the name of the One who is dressed in a robe dipped in blood? (Revelation 19:13)

A. The wrath of God
B. Everlasting of Everlasting
C. The Great Conqueror
D. The Word of God

122. Which of the following is correct about the One whose robe is dipped in blood? (Revelation 19: 14-16)

A. The armies of heaven follow Him, riding on white horses and dressed in fine linen, white and clean
B. A sharp sword comes from His mouth to strike the nations, and He will rule with an iron scepter
C. On His robe and His thigh is written: KING OF KINGS AND LORD OF LORDS
D. All the above

123. What will the birds flying in midair eat at the great supper of God? (Revelation 19: 17-18)

A. The spoils of battle and the weapons of the fallen armies
B. The flesh of kings, generals, mighty men, horses, and riders, and all people, free and slave, great and small
C. The souls of the wicked who refused to repent
D. The carcasses of the beasts and the false prophet

WEEK 6 MEMORY VERSE: REVELATION 22:12
And behold, I am coming quickly, and My reward is with Me, to give to everyone according to his work.

WEEK 6

124. What will happen when the beast, the kings of the earth, and their armies gather to fight the rider on the horse? (Revelation 19:19–21)

A. The beast and the false prophet will be captured—those who deceived many with signs and miracles
B. They will be thrown alive into the lake of burning sulfur
C. The rest will be killed by the sword that comes from the mouth of the rider on the horse, and the birds will feast on their flesh
D. All the above

125. What will happen to the dragon, that ancient serpent who is the devil, or Satan when the angel comes out of heaven with a key to the Abyss and with a great chain? (Revelation 20: 1-3)

A. He will be thrown into the eternal lake of fire which is the second death
B. He will be thrown into the Abyss for a thousand years, and then after that be released for a short time
C. He will be chained down and locked under the great river Euphrates with the four fallen angels
D. He will fight the angel and be thrown down to earth like lightning

126. Who did John see seated on thrones? (Revelation 20: 4)

A. Those who had been given authority to judge
B. Those who did not worship idols while they were on earth
C. Those who were dressed in white linen for their pure hearts
D. Those who had been rejected by the beast and the false prophet

WEEK 6 MEMORY VERSE: REVELATION 22:12
And behold, I am coming quickly, and My reward is with Me, to give to everyone according to his work.

> "I shall declare a thing, and it will be established for me (Job 22:28)"

Great job completing the week!

Did you memorize the daily verse?
Test yourself by writing it here...

_____

_____

_____

_____

_____

_____

Use this space to draw a scene from the Bible or reflect
on something you learned, felt or experienced...

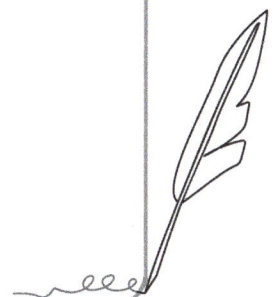

127. Who will come to life and reign with Christ for a thousand years? (Revelation 20:4)

A. Those who were beheaded for their testimony about Jesus and the Word of God
B. Those who refused to worship the beast or receive his mark
C. Those who were ready to face judgment
D. A and B are correct

128. When will the rest of the dead that do not rise in the first resurrection come to life? (Revelation 20:5-6)

A. When Jesus comes back riding on a white horse
B. After the thousand years are over
C. During the rapture
D. At the general resurrection of all the righteous.

129. Complete this verse: Blessed and holy are those who share in the first resurrection _____ (Revelation 20:6)

A. The second death has no power over them, but they will be priests of God and Christ and will reign with Him for a thousand years.
B. They will rule the nations and trample over the powers of Satan.
C. Their bodies will be glorified and not see decay, and they will rule with Christ eternally
D. For they will see God and will receive the crown with precious stones

WEEK 7 MEMORY VERSE: REVELATION 22:17
And the Spirit and the bride say, 'Come!' And let him who hears say, 'Come!' And let him who thirsts come. Whoever desires, let him take the water of life freely.

WEEK 7

130. What will happen after the thousand years are over? (Revelation 20:7–8)

A. Satan will be released from his prison
B. Satan will go out to deceive the nations in the four corners of the earth – Gog and Magog
C. Many people, like the sand on the seashore, will gather for battle
D. All the above

131. What will happen to the armies that surround the camp of God's people? (Revelation 20: 9-10)

A. The Lord will strike them with blindness, and they will wander in confusion
B. Their weapons will fail them, and they will flee
C. Fire will come down from heaven and consume them
D. The walls of the camp of God will rise like the walls of Jericho

132. Where will Satan spend eternity? (Revelation 20: 10)

A. He will be thrown in the lake of burning sulfur, where the beast and the prophet were thrown
B. He will be tormented day and night forever and ever
C. He will be hidden in darkness until the end of time
D. Only A and B are correct

WEEK 7 MEMORY VERSE: REVELATION 22:17
And the Spirit and the bride say, 'Come!' And let him who hears say, 'Come!' And let him who thirsts come. Whoever desires, let him take the water of life freely.

WEEK 7

133. Why was there no place found for the earth and the heavens? (Revelations 20: 11)

A. Because they fled from the presence of the One seated on the great white throne
B. Because a new heaven and earth had been created
C. Because they were judged and thrown into the lake of fire
D. Because wickedness had filled them like in the days of Noah

134. How will the dead be judged? (Revelation 20: 12)

A. By two witnesses and the law of Moses
B. Based on what they had done that is recorded in their books
C. By the mark of the beast that was on their forehead or their hand
D. By the 12 disciples of Jesus and the 12 tribes of Israel

135. The lake of fire is the second death. Who will be thrown into it? (Revelation 20:14–15)

A. Only Satan and the demons
B. Only those who worshiped the beast
C. Death, Hades, and anyone whose name is not written in the Lamb's Book of Life
D. Those who broke the Ten Commandments

WEEK 7 MEMORY VERSE: REVELATION 22:17
And the Spirit and the bride say, 'Come!' And let him who hears say, 'Come!' And let him who thirsts come. Whoever desires, let him take the water of life freely.

WEEK 7

136. What will pass away to make room for the new heaven and new earth? (Revelation 21:1)

A. The first heaven and the first earth
B. The first heaven, the first earth, and the sea
C. The beast, the false prophet, and the devil
D. Sin, death, and the grave

137. What did John see coming down from heaven like a beautifully dressed bride? (Revelation 21:2)

A. The church and the body of Christ
B. The Holy City, the New Jerusalem
C. The angel armies of God
D. The redeemed saints with crowns of gold

138. Where will God's new dwelling place be? (Revelation 21:3)

A. In the heavens with the angels
B. In the third heaven, far above the earth
C. Among His people - He will dwell with them
D. In the hearts of His prophets

WEEK 7 MEMORY VERSE: REVELATION 22:17
And the Spirit and the bride say, 'Come!' And let him who hears say, 'Come!' And let him who thirsts come. Whoever desires, let him take the water of life freely.

WEEK 7

139. What will be different when the old order of things pass away? (Revelation 21:4)

A. There will be no more death, mourning, crying, or pain
B. The world will have one currency and no more war
C. The sun and moon will stop shining
D. God will rewrite the laws of the world

140. What does it mean that Jesus is the Alpha and the Omega? (Revelation 21:6)

A. He is the most powerful King of all time
B. He is the Judge of the world
C. He is the Beginning and the End
D. These are the first and last letters of the Greek alphabet

141. What will happen to the cowardly, the unbelieving, the corrupt, the murderers, the sexually immoral, those who practice magic arts/witchcraft, the idol worshipers, and all liars? (Revelation 21:8)

A. God will look at their good deeds and decide if they should enter heaven
B. They will be forgiven if their sins are not too many
C. They will face the second death in the lake of fire and burning sulfur
D. They will be given one more chance to turn to God

WEEK 7 MEMORY VERSE: REVELATION 22:17
And the Spirit and the bride say, 'Come!' And let him who hears say, 'Come!' And let him who thirsts come. Whoever desires, let him take the water of life freely.

WEEK 7

142. Which of the following describes the Holy City, the New Jerusalem? (Revelation 21: 10-14)

A. It shines with the glory of God, like Jasper, clear as crystal
B. It has a high wall with twelve gates, 3 on each side, with 12 angels at the gates and the names of the twelve tribes of Israel
C. The wall of the city has twelve foundations, and on them are the names of the twelve disciples
D. All the above

143. What shape is the Holy City of Jerusalem? (Revelation 21: 15-16)

A. A rectangle
B. A Square (its length, width, and height are equal)
C. A triangle
D. A circle

144. Which of the following is NOT true about the Holy City of Jerusalem? (Revelation 21:18-21)

A. Its wall is made of jasper, and the city is made of pure gold
B. Each of its twelve gates is made of a single pearl
C. The streets are made of gold as clear as glass
D. The gates are made of bronze and guarded by mighty warriors

WEEK 7 MEMORY VERSE: REVELATION 22:17
And the Spirit and the bride say, 'Come!' And let him who hears say, 'Come!' And let him who thirsts come. Whoever desires, let him take the water of life freely.

WEEK 7

145. Why is there no temple, or sun, or moon, in the Holy City of Jerusalem? (Revelation 21: 22-24)

A. Because the sun and moon are no longer needed

B. Because the Lord God Almighty and the Lamb are its temple, and the glory of God gives it light

C. Because the angels will be the new source of light

D. Because the people will worship only in their hearts

146. Which of the following is NOT true about the Holy City of Jerusalem? (Revelation 21: 24-27)

A. The glory and honor of the nations will be brought into it

B. The gates will never be shut, because there is no night

C. Anyone can enter the city, even if their name is not in the Lamb's Book of Life

D. Nothing unclean or shameful will ever enter it

147. How often does the Tree of Life that is planted by the river of the water of life produce fruits? (Revelation 22:1-2)

A. Once a year

B. Every season

C. Every month

D. Once in eternity

WEEK 7 MEMORY VERSE: REVELATION 22:17

And the Spirit and the bride say, 'Come!' And let him who hears say, 'Come!' And let him who thirsts come. Whoever desires, let him take the water of life freely.

BONUS QUESTIONS

148. What are the leaves on the Tree of Life used for? (Revelation 22:2)

A. To provide food for angels
B. To decorate the city
C. To bring healing to the nations
D. To give shade in the garden

149. Should people worship angels? (Revelation 22: 8-9)

A. Yes, because angels are holy
B. No, because angels are fellow servants of God
C. Only archangels can be worshipped
D. Yes, but only in heaven

150. Why did the angel tell John not to seal up the words of the prophecy? (Revelation 22:10)

A. Because the time of Jesus' return is near
B. Because John needed to memorize them
C. Because the scroll could not be sealed
D. Because John was not finished writing

WEEK 7 MEMORY VERSE: REVELATION 22:17
And the Spirit and the bride say, 'Come!' And let him who hears say, 'Come!' And let him who thirsts come. Whoever desires, let him take the water of life freely.

BONUS QUESTIONS

151. How will Jesus reward each person when He returns?
(Revelation 22:12)

A. According to how long each person has been a Christian and a follower of Jesus
B. According to age, older people are expected to have done more
C. According to each person's deeds (actions)
D. According to each person's good intentions

152. Who will be outside the gates of the Holy City?
(Revelation 22:15)

A. Only those who were unkind
B. Those who practice witchcraft, sin, or love lies
C. Those who don't believe in angels
D. No one, because everyone is welcome

153. Who sent the angel to share this prophecy with the churches?
(Revelation 22:16)

A. The apostle John
B. Jesus, the Root and Offspring of David, the Bright Morning Star
C. The prophet Elijah
D. The archangel Michael

WEEK 7 MEMORY VERSE: REVELATION 22:17
And the Spirit and the bride say, 'Come!' And let him who hears say, 'Come!' And let him who thirsts come. Whoever desires, let him take the water of life freely.

BONUS QUESTIONS

154. What does the Spirit and the bride say? (Revelation 22: 17)

A. Be ready!
B. Come!
C. Repent!
D. Believe!

155. What will happen to anyone who adds or removes words from the prophecy contained in the Book of Revelation? (Revelation 22: 19)

A. To those who add, God will add to them the plagues described in the Book of Revelation
B. To those who take away, God will take from them any share in the Tree of Life and the Holy City
C. None of the answers are correct
D. Both A and B

156. What are the final words of Jesus in the Book of Revelation? (Revelation 22:20)

A. "It is finished."
B. "Peace be with you."
C. "Yes, I am coming soon."
D. "Your will be done on earth as it is in heaven."

WEEK 7 MEMORY VERSE: REVELATION 22:17
And the Spirit and the bride say, 'Come!' And let him who hears say, 'Come!' And let him who thirsts come. Whoever desires, let him take the water of life freely.

> "But thanks be to God, who gives me the victory through our Lord Jesus Christ
> (1 Corinthians 15:57)"

Great job completing the week!

**Did you memorize the daily verse?
Test yourself by writing it here...**

_____

_____

_____

_____

_____

**Use this space to draw a scene from the Bible or reflect
on something you learned, felt or experienced...**

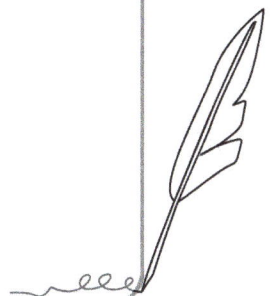

Certificate of Completion

This Certificate Certifies That:

_____

Has Successfully Completed The Revelation Workbook!

Flo & Grace

_____
PARENT/TEACHER SIGNATURE

PROJECT KINGDOM COME

WOULD YOU LIKE TO ACCEPT JESUS INTO YOUR HEART?

THE BIBLE SAYS:

If you confess with your mouth that Jesus is Lord and believe in your heart that God has raised Him from the dead, you will be saved
(Romans 10:9)

SAY THE PRAYER BELOW OUT LOUD AND BELIEVE IT IN YOUR HEART!

Dear Lord Jesus,
I know that I am a sinner, and I ask for Your forgiveness.
I believe You died for my sins and rose from the dead.
I repent of my sins and invite You to come into my heart and life.
I want to trust and follow You as my Lord and Savior. Help me to live for you for the rest of my life.
I am now a child of God, and I ask You to fill me with Your Holy Spirit.

In Jesus' Name I pray, Amen.

Congratulations!
If you have prayed this prayer, please let an adult know or send an email to mybibleworkbooks@gmail.com

ANSWER KEY:

<<<<< **ANSWER KEY:** >>>>>

1. C
2. A
3. C
4. D
5. B
6. A
7. D
8. D
9. B
10. C
11. A
12. D

13. D
14. B
15. A
16. C
17. C
18. D
19. D
20. B
21. B
22. B
23. D
24. A

25. B
26. C
27. D
28. B
29. A
30. C
31. D
32. D
33. D
34. A
35. B
36. A

37. C	49. D	61. C
38. D	50. A	62. D
39. C	51. B	63. B
40. B	52. C	64. C
41. A	53. D	65. D
42. D	54. B	66. B
43. C	55. B	67. B
44. A	56. D	68. A
45. D	57. A	69. A
46. B	58. C	70. C
47. C	59. B	71. D
48. D	60. C	72. C

73. B	85. D	97. B
74. C	86. C	98. D
75. C	87. B	99. C
76. C	88. C	100. D
77. C	89. D	101. D
78. D	90. C	102. B
79. D	91. A	103. A
80. D	92. B	104. B
81. D	93. A	105. D
82. A	94. A	106. A
83. A	95. B	107. D
84. D	96. C	108. B

109. C	121. D	133. A
110. A	122. D	134. B
111. D	123. B	135. C
112. A	124. D	136. B
113. D	125. B	137. B
114. D	126. A	138. C
115. A	127. D	139. A
116. B	128. B	140. C
117. C	129. A	141. C
118. D	130. D	142. D
119. B	131. C	143. B
120. B	132. D	144. D

145. B

146. C

147. C

148. C

149. B

150. A

151. C

152. B

153. B

154. B

155. D

156. C

PLEASE GIVE US YOUR FEEDBACK!

Please send us your feedback on this workbook. We would love to hear what you enjoyed most, and ways you think it could be improved!

Please Send an email to: MyBibleWorkbooks@gmail.com, or leave us a comment on one of our social media pages.

MyBibleWorkbooks@gmail.com

Projectkingdomcome

Projectkingdomcome

SCAN ME

"

And I am certain that God, who began the good work within you, will continue His work until it is finally finished on the day when Christ Jesus returns. Philippians 1:6

"

DRAW HERE

DRAW HERE

DRAW HERE

DRAW HERE